Classics to Moderns
Compiled and edited by Denes Agay

Each of the six volumes in the Classics to Moderns series presents a panorama of keyboard music from early Baroque to the present. Selections are in their original forms, neither re-arranged nor simplified. In all the books the pieces appear in approximately chronological order, but the listing of contents follows a graded sequence and each book is a little more difficult than the one before it. In this way the player can make sure progress to the pieces in Book 6.

In the music of the pre-classic period marks of tempo, phrasing and expression are often editorial additions. These signs were supplied for a quicker and easier understanding of the structure and mood of the composition. They are to be considered as suggestions rather than rigid directions.

Yorktown Music Press

This book © copyright 1977 by
Yorktown Music Press

Exclusive Distributors:
Hal Leonard
7777 West Bluemound Road, Milwaukee, WI 53213
Email: info@halleonard.com

Hal Leonard Europe Limited
42 Wigmore Street Marylebone, London, WIU 2 RY
Email: info@halleonardeurope.com

Hal Leonard Australia Pty. Ltd.
4 Lentara Court Cheltenham, Victoria 9132, Australia
Email: info@halleonard.com.au

For all works contained herein: Unauthorized copying, arranging, adapting,
recording, Internet posting, public performance, or other distribution of
the music in this publication is an infringement of copyright.
Infringers are liable under the law.

ISBN.0.86001.408.8
YK 20063

www.halleonard.com

Contents

(in graded sequence)

Fantasia	George Frideric Handel	(1685–1759)	4
Viennese Sonata No. 1 *First Movement*	Wolfgang Amadeus Mozart	(1756–1791)	10
Two Waltzes	Johannes Brahms	(1833–1897)	18
Spanish Dance	Enrique Granados	(1867–1916)	23
Solfeggietto	Carl Philipp Emanuel Bach	(1714–1788)	8
Sonata	Domenico Scarlatti	(1685–1757)	6
Moment Musical	Franz Schubert	(1797–1828)	16
Bagatelle (*C minor*)	Ludwig van Beethoven	(1770–1827)	12
The Elf	Robert Schumann	(1810–1856)	15
Nocturne (*C-sharp minor*)	Frédéric Chopin	(1810–1849)	20
Prelude	Dmitri Kabalevsky	(1904–)	26
Golliwog's Cake-Walk	Claude Debussy	(1862–1918)	28

Fantasia

George Frideric Handel

Sonata

Domenico Scarlatti

Solfeggietto

Carl Philipp Emanuel Bach

© 1962 Consolidated Music Publishers, Inc.

Viennese Sonatina No. 1
First Movement

Wolfgang Amadeus Mozart

© 1962 Consolidated Music Publishers, Inc.

Bagatelle

Ludwig van Beethoven

The Elf
Op. 127, No. 17

Robert Schumann

So schnell als möglich
(As fast as possible)

© 1969 Consolidated Music Publishers, Inc.

Moment Musical
Op. 94, No. 5

Allegro vivace

Franz Schubert

© 1969 Consolidated Music Publishers, Inc.

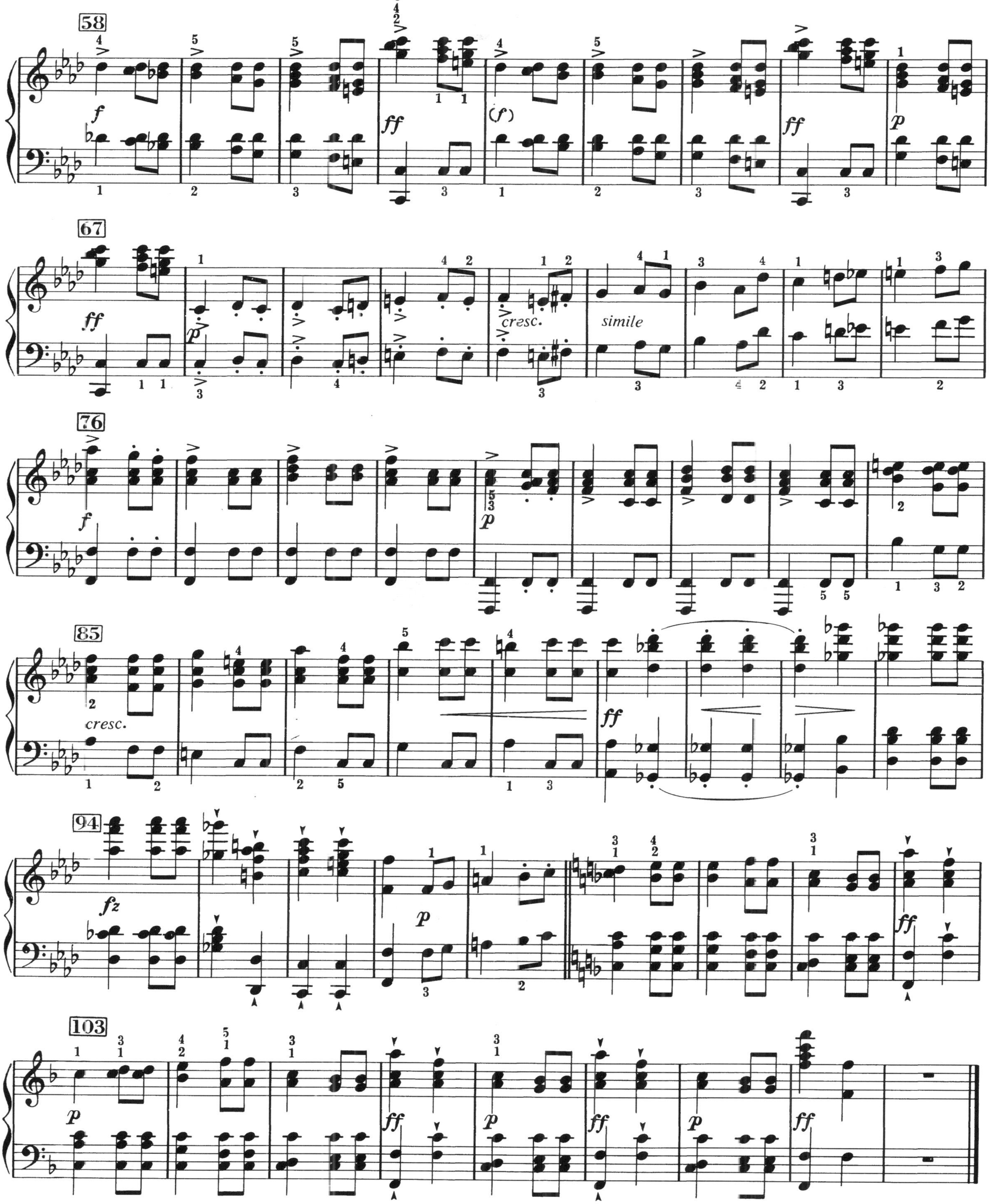
58
67
cresc.
simile
76
85
cresc.
94
103

Two Waltzes
Op. 39, No's. 1. 2.

1.

Johannes Brahms

© 1969 Consolidated Music Publishers, Inc.

2.

Nocturne
Op. Posth.

Frédéric Chopin

© 1976 Yorktown Music Press, Inc.

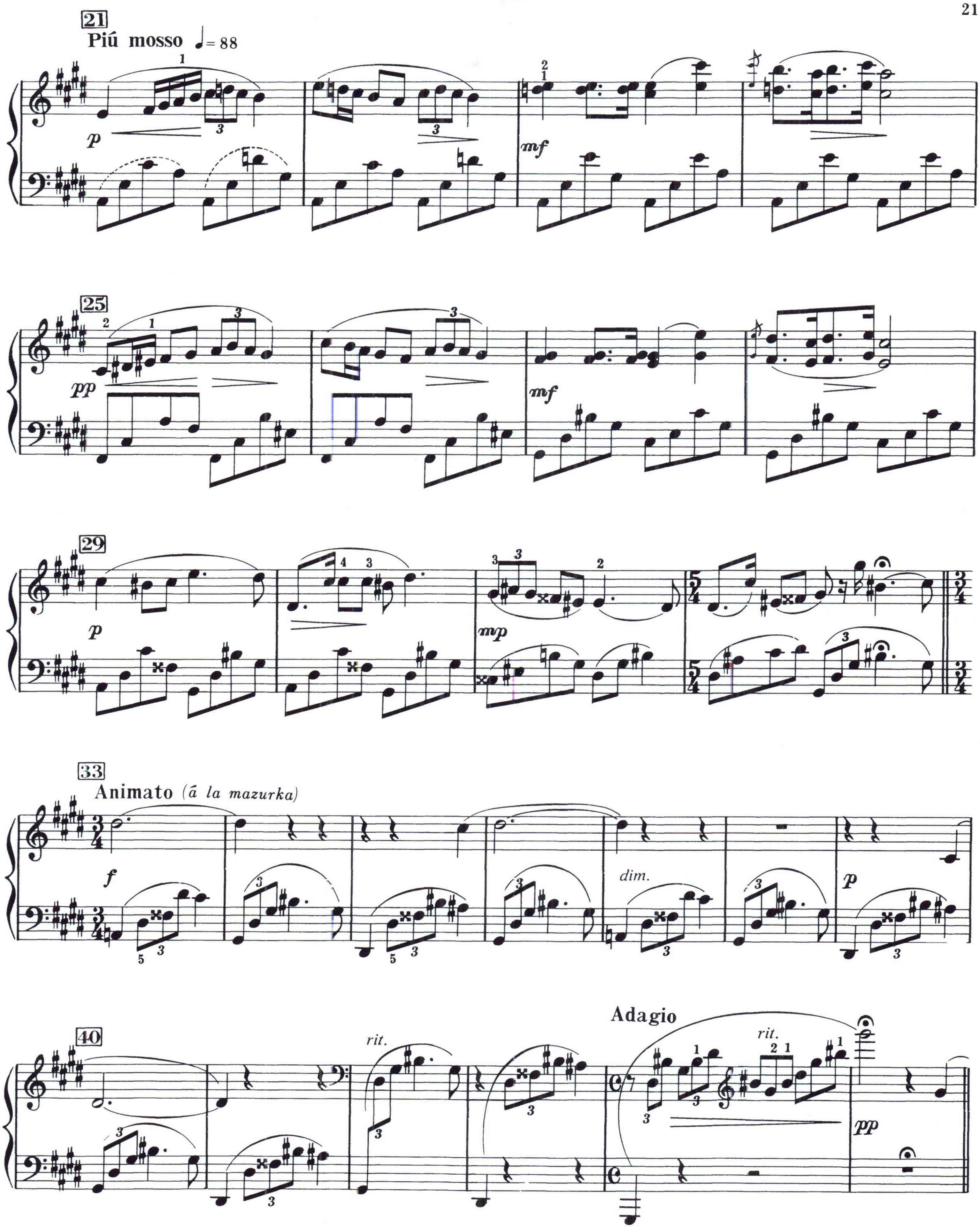
21
Piú mosso ♩= 88
p
mf
25
pp
mf
29
p
mp
33
Animato (á la mazurka)
f
dim.
p
40
rit.
Adagio
rit.
pp

Spanish Dance
"Minueto" from "Danzas Espanoles", Op. 5

Enrique Granados

© 1969 Consolidated Music Publishers, Inc.

Prelude

Op. 38, No. 2

Dmitri Kabalevsky

© 1969 Consolidated Music Publishers, Inc.

Golliwog's Cake-Walk
from "Children's Corner"

Claude Debussy